City of Rochester

William A. Johnson, Jr.
Mayor

City Hall, Room 307-A
30 Church Street
Rochester, New York 14614-1284
(716) 428-7045

FAX (716) 428-6059
TDD/Voice 232-3260

Jordan African-American Sites Committee
c/o The Landmark Society of
Western New York
133 South Fitzhugh Street
Rochester, New York 14608

Dear Friends:

On behalf of the citizens of Rochester, I would like to congratulate the members of the Jordan African-American Historic Sites Committee for undertaking this important project. This publication documents the distinguished record of accomplishment by local African-Americans. *The City of Frederick Douglass: Rochester's African-American People and Places* is truly a landmark account of the many historical contributions blacks have made to the growth and prosperity of the City of Rochester and County of Monroe.

Many of us are familiar with the more prominent African-American men and women who have helped make this a thriving metropolitan region. There are, however, hundreds of others who have received little or no recognition for their significant contributions to local history. This project corrects many of these omissions, by preserving the achievements of local blacks in published form.

I would like to especially thank committee chair, Katherine Jordan, whose guidance and direction made this project possible, and Eugene DuBois, whose extensive research and writing made this publication a reality. The cooperative support of staff members from the Landmark Society of Western New York; Rochester Museum and Science Center; Rochester Public Library; and other individuals too numerous to mention, is also very much appreciated.

Finally, it is my hope that all of the local school districts in the area will find ways to incorporate this publication into their local history curricula. This will ensure that future generations are aware of the tremendous impact African-Americans have made to the Community of Monroe.

Again, congratulations to everyone who assisted in making this publication possible.

Sincerely,

William A. Johnson, Jr.
Mayor

EEO Employer/Handicapped

Table of Contents

Foreword

My thanks to the Jordan African-American Historic Sites Committee for its work both as individuals and as a group in bringing our dream, *The City of Frederick Douglass: Rochester's African-American People and Places*, to fruition. The idea of a printed history depicting individuals and sites significant to African-Americans of the Rochester area easily could have been a dream deferred, "dried up like a raisin in the sun." Instead, here it is for all of Rochester to read and enjoy.

Our committee meetings were wonderful events of discovery which have expanded my own knowledge considerably. The committee's disciplined approach as historians and writers made this a reality. Thanks also to staff of the Landmark Society for its professional expertise. Thanks especially to Henry McCartney, Society executive director for guidance, direction. and sincere interest in this project.

Now to toss out another committee dream as articulated by Mary Jo Barone — that this project evolve into a school curriculum so that Rochester area children could learn of the contributions of all of their forefathers and mothers. Then to dream on, maybe we could enlarge upon *The City of Frederick Douglass: Rochester's African-American People and Places*, making it into a comprehensive local history which both children and adults could enjoy.

Katherine Jordan, chair.

From the Publisher...

The Landmark Society is extremely pleased to serve as this book's publisher. This work is another step in what needs to be an on-going process to identify African-American achievements. The personalities, sites and institutions presented here have been selected to portray the history of the African-American community from its earliest days to just after World War II.

This work's approach and space limitations means that many important people and facts could not be included. Further, more needs to be known and we welcome whatever additional information our readers may have about Rochester's African-American past.

Historic preservation comes alive when people have a passion for identifying, publicizing and protecting historic resources that are important to them. Kay Jordan and the Jordan African-American Historic Sites Committee has that passion and that passion is infectious. Their knowledge and hard work is what has made this book possible.

The Landmark Society is also grateful to those who have provided financial support. The New York State Council on the Arts has supported this work and earlier research by the committee. The National Trust for Historic Preservation has helped both with a grant and with scholarships to bring committee members to its annual conference. In addition, we are grateful to have Thomas James Associates as our corporate sponsor. This publication also benefited from the generosity of an anonymous donor.

We hope you enjoy and benefit from reading *The City of Frederick Douglass: Rochester's African-American People and Places*.

Henry McCartney
Executive Director
The Landmark Society of Western New York

Acknowledgments

Many individuals and institutions have contributed to this historic and landmark effort. The members of the Jordan African-American Historic Sites Committee, which began a successful effort to have the Dr. Anthony L. Jordan home at 136 Adams Street declared a city landmark, was most valuable. Committee chair, Katherine Jordan, kept the author focused, and provided hours of research and editing assistance.

Victoria Schmidt and Lee Kemp, of the Rochester Museum and Science Center, were helpful in opening the museum's resources. Betty Schmidt of the Friends of Mount Hope Cemetery assisted in locating burial sites and historic information regarding the final resting places of many individuals.

Ira Srole, photographer for the City of Rochester, and Lewis Bracey, the Rochester Museum & Science Center's Stone Negative Collection and Charles Price, Charles Frazier and Millard E. Latimer, Jr., provided photos.

The *Democrat and Chronicle* and the *Times-Union* created the maps used in this publication.

The staff of the Local History Division of the Rochester Public Library and the volunteer staff of the Scottsville Free Library helped in locating resources and making available their extensive photographic and newspaper files.

Special appreciation is extended to Flo Paxson for her editing assistance, and for sharing her computer skills with one far less proficient.

Thanks also to Cathy Rourke for expertly typing and editing the many drafts and coordinating the various committee activities and meetings.

Lastly, this author and the committee are grateful to Henry McCartney for his enthusiastic dedication to and support of the project.

Eugene E. Du Bois

About the author...

Eugene E. Du Bois was born in Rochester, New York. He graduated from Madison High School on the West Side. He received his A.B. degree from Hillsdale College (Michigan), the M.S. degree from Boston University, and the Ed.D. degree from Wayne State University in Detroit.

He has served as Administrative Assistant to the President of Monroe Community College in Rochester, and on the faculties of Boston University, Nova University, The George Washington University, and Northeastern University.

Dr. Du Bois has been a visiting professor at a number of institutions including: Rhode Island College, the University of the District of Columbia, and the State University of Utrecht in the Netherlands. He was a W.K. Kellogg Fellow, and is the author of numerous articles and studies. In 1990 he published: *The Urban Black Church and the Changing Metropolis.*

Photo, Andy Olenick

The Jordan African-American Historic Sites Committee in the lobby of the Hochstein Music School—(left to right) front row: Katherine Jordan, Eugene E. Du Bois; second row: Lewis Bracey, Henry McCartney, Anna Bibbs-Rodriguez, Charles Frazier, Charles Price, LiAni Lewis; balcony: Robin Nowell, Cindy Boyer, Loretta Scott, J.Ernest Du Bois, Flo Paxson.

The City of Frederick Douglass: Rochester's African-American People and Places

Few if any of the ethnic groups that have contributed to Rochester's growth can match the Negroes in the dramatic quality of their local history. They have from the first produced striking and often distinguished leaders.
—Blake McKelvey, Rochester City Historian 1948-1973

The history of the African-American experience in Rochester and the Genesee Valley is one of migration, discrimination, self-help, community support, and the ability to overcome challenges unimaginable to most Americans. Rochester was able to attract and support an outstanding leader of his era, Frederick Douglass, and others who have made outstanding contributions to their city, region and nation.

Rochester's early history is also told by many unsung African-American citizens whose early efforts built and supported the neighborhoods, the churches, and other institutions that have nourished Rochester's African-American community.

In some respects, the Rochester experience is unique among American metropolitan areas. There were black settlers in what became Monroe County before Europeans, Southerners, New Englanders, and other groups settled in great numbers in the Valley of the Genesee. These settlers included explorers, frontiersmen, and slaves. However, the African-American population of the area now known as Rochester and Monroe County has, until recently, been rather small.

According to the U.S. Census of 1820, 28 blacks resided in Rochesterville. After the Civil War (1870) the number increased to 427. The earliest large migration to the area after the Civil War brought people from Culpeper, VA, to Mumford, NY in rural Monroe County. It was not until 1920 that the number exceeded one thousand (1,579) or 0.5 % of Rochester's population.

Rochester's African-American population increased slightly after World War I, but not nearly as much as the population of other industrial cities such as Detroit, Chicago and Pittsburgh. Blacks, who migrated to these cities with heavy industries requiring large numbers of unskilled laborers, found a more hospitable reception from the leaders of business and commerce. Rochester's African-Americans were relegated to the low-paying menial jobs of elevator operators, janitors, porters, chauffeurs and domestics. In the face of these odds, they survived, raised and educated their children, and built religious and social institutions.

This book focuses on those African-Americans who came to Rochester before World War II and built a community for those who came after. It is also designed to identify the buildings and places that signify the enduring presence of a black community in Rochester with its own history, culture and traditions.

The book is divided into five sections:

The Downtown section may serve as a self-guided walking tour to points of interest in the history of Rochester's black community. Between the Austin Steward marker at East Main and St. Paul Streets, and the Steward display on the mezzanine level of the Holiday Inn to the Isaac and Amy Post House marker at the Hochstein Music School at North Plymouth Ave. and Church St., a short review of early African-American history may be observed on both sides of Main St.

The West Side is the largest and most varied, in terms of architecture, lifestyles and mix. Rochester's first residential neighborhood, called Corn Hill, is on the West Side. The West Side is historically significant not only to the black community but to all residents of Rochester as well. To celebrate the contributions of African-Americans who lived in the West Side, this section takes you to Corn

Hill; the rest of the Third Ward; and the 19th Ward, on the city's extreme southwest.

The Southeast is interesting primarily because the Frederick Douglass Square area, with his statue and nearby home site, and Mount Hope Cemetery are located here. The cemetery includes the remains of early black residents, as well as more contemporary people who have contributed to the Rochester community.

The Northeast traditionally has been the point of entry for a variety of new Rochester residents. While the earliest African-Americans settled in the Third Ward, near the homes of the wealthy millers, merchants, and professionals, later arrivals who settled in the northeast joined ethnic groups already in Rochester. As the earlier settlers moved on, African-Americans began to dominate this community.

The Migrants: From Culpeper, VA, and Sanford, FL, to Rural Rochester. This section covers two early migrations: the first to the Mumford and Caledonia areas by post-Civil War area residents of Culpeper, Virginia; the second, the Depression-era migration of people from Sanford, Florida.

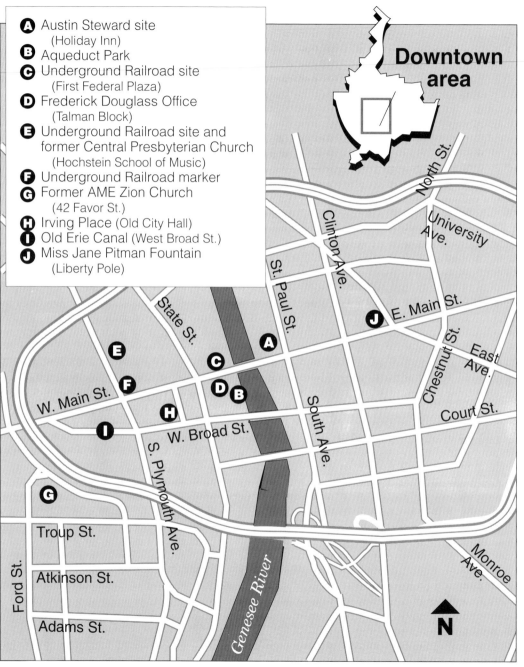

Ⓐ Austin Steward site
   (Holiday Inn)
Ⓑ Aqueduct Park
Ⓒ Underground Railroad site
   (First Federal Plaza)
Ⓓ Frederick Douglass Office
   (Talman Block)
Ⓔ Underground Railroad site and
   former Central Presbyterian Church
   (Hochstein School of Music)
Ⓕ Underground Railroad marker
Ⓖ Former AME Zion Church
   (42 Favor St.)
Ⓗ Irving Place (Old City Hall)
Ⓘ Old Erie Canal (West Broad St.)
Ⓙ Miss Jane Pitman Fountain
   (Liberty Pole)

Downtown area

North St.

University Ave.

Clinton Ave.

St. Paul St.

State St.

Ⓔ
Ⓕ
Ⓒ
Ⓐ
Ⓓ Ⓑ
Ⓗ
Ⓘ
Ⓙ E. Main St.

W. Main St.

Chestnut St.

East Ave.

Court St.

W. Broad St.

South Ave.

S. Plymouth Ave.

Ⓖ

Troup St.

Ford St.

Atkinson St.

Adams St.

Genesee River

Monroe Ave.

N

Map courtesy of the Democrat and Chronicle and Times-Union

Downtown: Explorers, Slaves, Freemen and Leaders

Aqueduct Park, on the edge of the Genesee River, and at the corner of West Main St. and Graves Ave., is an appropriate starting point to visit historic Rochester. It was here, on the Genesee River, that the natural "Falls of the Genesee," the area's early name, gave birth to America's first boomtown. On this spot, it is still possible to imagine Rochester as it once was, a part of the American frontier.

African-Americans were among the early explorers and settlers of the upper Genesee Valley. The first may have been Captain Sunfish, an escaped slave who came to the Genesee Region during the Revolutionary War. He lived with the Senecas, took a Native American wife, became a successful trader and eventually settled in Tonawanda. A daughter became one of the many wives of Ebenezer "Indian" Allan, Rochester's notorious first settler who established a mill on the west bank of the Genesee. Some African-American families in western New York can trace their roots to Captain Sunfish and Ebenezer Allan.

Courtesy of the City of Rochester

The Genesee River Waterfalls powered the industries that made Rochester America's first boomtown.

It is a short walk to 39 West Main St., where, in the Monroe County Office building, two 1788 millstones or grist wheels, used by Ebenezer "Indian" Allan, are on display. Rochester's early milling industry bestowed on it the sobriquet, the "Flour City." The wheels may be found on the west wall of the second-floor level of the atrium.

Another early frontiersman was an African-American named Asa Dunbar. In 1794, he opened the first clearing and was for a while the only settler at the Indian Landing, an outlet of Irondequoit Bay, now in Ellison Park. He resided in the area for many years, where he mined salt and had a farm and perhaps a tavern on what is now N. Winton Road. Other early African-American pioneers were escaped slaves who gravitated to the frontier. Concerned about their freedom, they unfortunately did not establish permanent residences nor leave other enduring records.

When Colonel Nathaniel Rochester traveled north to settle in New York State, he brought along his slaves from Maryland. Settling first in Dansville, New York, he manumitted his slaves, and these African-Americans moved with him in 1818 to what became Rochesterville.

Austin Steward (1793-1869).

Slavery, however, remained legal in New York Sate. It is believed that there were as many as a dozen slaves living in Rochesterville as early as 1812, nine years before Monroe became a county. The birth of a child to slaves was recorded on December 15, 1812, the only official record of slavery in what is now Monroe County. Titus Lord, purchased in 1813, was the slave of Caleb Hopkins of Pittsford. Hopkins purchased another slave in 1815.

In 1817, more than 20 years after the signing of the United States Constitution, the New York State Legislature dealt with slavery by signing legislation that declared that slaves born prior to July 4, 1799, would be free as of July 4, 1827.

However, children of slaves born during the interim (July 4, 1799, to July 4, 1827) were not free. They still owed a period of service to their masters. Thus, some form of slavery existed after the general emancipation of 1827.

Austin Steward: East across the historic Main St. bridge, built in 1857, stands the Holiday Inn. This is the location of one of the city's first black-owned businesses. Austin Steward, a fugitive slave, is considered one of Rochester's first African-American businessmen.

Steward was born into slavery in Prince William County, VA, in 1793. He was brought into New York State by his master and was often hired out to local farmers to supplement the income of his owner, Capt. William Helm, who had experienced severe financial losses. Steward found sympathetic friends, especially Dennis Comstock, president of the New York Manumission Society, and his brother, Otis, with whom he lived. It was during this period that Steward attended the Academy in Farmington, NY for three winters, although he was now 23 years old. Steward opened a meat market in September, 1817, and in 1818 he purchased land on E. Main St. on which he built a two-story dwelling. Life was not easy. Early on his competitors would tear down his sign or destroy it by painting it black. However, Steward prospered and became a leading supplier to the homes of established families.

As an active member of the African-American community, he helped to establish The Sabbath School for Coloreds. He served as a trustee of the African Methodist Church and wrote and lectured on social, economic, and political equality. He also became active in the abolitionist movement, helping to establish the Wilberforce Colony, a community of former slaves, in Canada. This experimental colony was unsuccessful. A believer in temperance, he refused to sell alcohol in his store. As a tribute to his success and prominence in the community, on July 5, 1827, Steward was invited to deliver Rochester's New York Emancipation Day speech, to mark the end of slavery in New York State.

Having lived in New York and been hired out, Steward assumed that he was free and that Helm had forfeited his claim. However, Helm continued to assert his claim. Eventually, he begrudgingly granted Steward his freedom. In later years, Steward wrote his autobiography, *Twenty-two Years a Slave and Forty Years a Freeman*.

A commemorative bust of Austin Steward and a historical display are located on the mezzanine level of the Holiday Inn. A pedestrian historical marker is near the northwest corner of East Main St. and St. Paul St.

Austin Steward wrote in his autobiography about Doctor Davis, a fugitive slave from Kentucky. Davis apparently learned his craft from his owner and practiced in early Rochesterville. Two agents, seeking the fugitive, apprehended Davis, and he was arrested and bound over for trial.

The court appearance was crowded with spectators. As the trial proceeded, the black men of the village were able to seize Davis and disguise him in new clothes while the court officers stood near the door. With this ruse, Davis was quickly removed from the court and placed on a packet boat for Buffalo.

After the loss of the fugitive slave, handbills were printed and distributed offering $50.00 for his recapture. Some of these handbills were thrown onto the boat carrying Dr. Davis. Soon recognized, he was dragged from the boat and returned to the Kentucky agents.

Struggling against his recapture and return to slavery, Davis produced a razor and slit his throat. The town authorities, fearful that medical care and expenses would be extensive, requested security and indemnity from the agents. Believing Davis dead, the agents returned to Kentucky without him. Davis, however, recovered after a period. He returned to Rochester and later received assistance to move to Canada. Austin Steward wrote:

"I have often heard from him during his residence in that country, where no slaves exist and he has done well, having quite an extensive practice in medicine . . ."

Underground Railroad. Rochester, with its prime location on Lake Ontario and close to Canada, became an important location for the underground railroad. Beginning in the 1830s the underground railroad became a significant part of Rochester's abolitionist activities.

The Fugitive Slave Law of 1793 was a strong incentive to capture fugitives and to return them to their owners. However, the later 1850 law was even stronger. This legislation provided for a $1,000 fine and an additional $1,000 for each fugitive assisted to fleeing, plus a five-year term of imprisonment. This 1850 law was devastating to Rochester's African-American community. One author documented that from one church alone, 112 members of 118 members of the Abyssinian Baptist Church, including the pastor, fled to Canada.

Rochester citizens provided shelter in Underground Railroad "stations" to fugitive slaves en route to freedom in Canada.

Courtesy of the City of Rochester

Both African-American and white Rochesterians defied these laws, and many homes in the Rochester area harbored fugitive slaves as they made their way north. At 12 Buffalo St., (now E. Main St.) the site of the present-day First Federal Plaza, Edward C. Williams operated a sail-manufacturing company in a loft. This building, a downtown station for slaves enroute to Canada, housed fugitive slaves prior to their sailing north to Canada. The loft was also used as a school to prepare fugitive slaves for a life of freedom.

Isaac and Amy Post, who lived near the northeast corner of W. Main and Plymouth Ave., were two of the many "conductors" on the Underground Railroad. One evening as many as 15 fugitive slaves found shelter in their home. The Posts' home was on the site now occupied by the Hochstein Music School, the former Central Presbyterian Church. In the church's large sanctuary, built in 1890, funeral services were held for both Frederick Douglass in 1895 and Susan B. Anthony in 1906. In front of the school and on the corner of W. Main and N. Plymouth Ave. are historical markers commemorating the Underground Railroad.

Frederick Douglass. Frederick Douglass is one of Rochester's most famous residents. His contribution to the abolitionist movement and the civil rights of African-Americans is unsurpassed. Born in 1818 (some sources say 1817) in Maryland, Douglass escaped slavery in 1838 and soon gained renown as an anti-slavery lecturer and writer.

From the late summer through October, 1842, Douglass lectured as an agent of the American Anti-Slavery Society. It was during this time that he toured western New York. On August 30 of that year Douglass spoke in Rochester for the first time. He was received at the home of Isaac and Amy Post.

This visit to what he believed to be a most progressive community influenced his decision to relocate to Rochester and to launch the *North Star* newspaper. Douglass arrived in 1847 and began publishing his newspaper in December in the A.M.E. Zion Church on Favor St. Later, Douglass opened an office in the center of Rochester's downtown at 25 Buffalo St. (now 25 E. Main St.) in what was called the Talman Block. It was from this building that he penned his editorials and met his many visitors, including John Brown prior to his raid at Harper's Ferry, Virginia, in 1859. In 1851, the newspaper was renamed *Frederick Douglass' Paper.* A plaque placed by Sigma Delta Chi, the professional journalists' society, marks this site. Frederick Douglass also was an important underground railroad conductor, as his fame attracted to his office runaway slaves who were desperately seeking assistance. (Across Main St., in front of Reynolds Arcade, a historic marker helps direct visitor's attention to this important downtown site.)

While in Rochester, Douglass also became active in the women's rights movement, attending the first women's rights convention (1848) held in Seneca Falls, NY, and later working closely with Susan B. Anthony.

The Talman Block has been significantly altered through the

Frederick Douglass

John Brown

13

The Talman Building retains the 19th-century facade from Douglass' era. In contrast, is the 20th-century skyscraper on E. Main St.

years. However, a walk down Aqueduct St. reveals an earlier stone facade and 19th-century design at the rear of the building. Still visible is the rough-faced stone block wall that extends up three stories (the fourth floor is brick, apparently a later addition). During Douglass' time, the back of the Talman Block faced the Erie Canal (now Broad St.) and Child's Basin, a docking area for canal packet boats immediately adjacent to the rear of this building. The nearby Broad St. Bridge (1920s) is built atop the Erie Canal aqueduct, a 19th-century engineering marvel built in 1842 to carry the canal over the Genesee River.

Rochester's former city hall (now Irving Place) was built next to the Erie Canal at Broad and S. Fitzhugh Sts. Here, Frederick Douglass was laid in state in 1895, his body having been returned to Rochester from Washington, D.C. School children in the higher grades were excused from classes to pay their respects.

The Talman Block also housed the Anti-Slavery Office and reading room maintained by William Jacobs, an agent for both the Massachusetts and New England Anti-Slavery Societies. The 1849-50 City Directory lists his sister, Harriet A. Jacobs, as an agent. While her brother, William, lectured for the societies, she lived at the Sophia St. (N. Plymouth Ave.) home of Isaac and Amy Post. A former slave, Mrs. Jacobs wrote, *Incidents in the Life of a Slave Girl*, which was published in 1861. This book, unlike other slave narratives of the time, describes the perils of female slaves, and became an early feminist documentary. Mrs. Jacobs remained in Rochester from March, 1849 to Sept., 1850.

Douglass was aided by **Jacob P. Morris** who maintained several barber shops in the downtown area, including one at 31 Buffalo St. (now 31 E. Main St.). Douglass, speaking about J. P. Morris and the Underground Railroad, wrote, "J. P. Morris and myself received and dispatched passengers from Rochester to Canada, where they were received by Rev. Hiram Wilson. When a party arrived in Rochester, it was the business of Mr. Morris and myself to raise funds with which to pay their passage to St. Catharines, and it is due to trust to state that we seldom called in vain upon Whig or Democrat for help. A community activist, Morris along with Steward and a W.H. Bishop, were appointed agents to look after the interests of the colored schools."

John Jenkins is first listed as a grocer in the Rochester City Directory of 1844. In 1847 he is listed as a physician. In 1851 Jenkins had an office over 39 Buffalo St. By the 19th-century the practice of medicine had not achieved the professional status we attribute to the modern healing arts. The practices of blood-letting and herbology were fairly common therapeutic procedures. So it is not at all surprising that Jenkins could move from being a grocer to a physician in a matter of a few years.

Dr. Jenkins, who had been a slave in Virginia, spent several years in Rochester working to purchase the freedom of his two daughters. He spent some 16 years in Rochester before moving to Canada after passage of the Fugitive Slave Law of 1850.

In 1838 Jenkins discovered his long-lost brother and learned that his two daughters, born in slavery, had been separated and sold further south. In 1855 he learned that his younger daughter was in Richmond. He paid a man to obtain her but he never saw the man or his money again.

Later he learned the name of his daughter's owner, Allen Y. Stokes. Stokes demanded $850 for her freedom, and in 1857 this daughter and her free husband joined Dr. Jenkins in Canada. The following year Jenkins learned that his elder daughter was living in Florida. She was the property of ex-Territorial Governor, Richard K. Call (1836-1839, 1844-1845). Call requested $400 as the purchase price for her freedom. He stated that she had been a good house servant and would only sell her to her father. In appreciation for her service the former governor gave her $50.00. Thus, this former Rochesterian reunited his family in Hamilton, Ontario, Canada, on November 4, 1858.

West Side area

Madison St.

Brown St.

W. Main St.

Ⓚ

Troup St. Ⓑ Ⓐ

490

Clifton St.

Ⓓ

Adams St. Ⓕ

Ⓖ Ⓔ

Tremont St. Ⓒ

Clarissa St.

Ⓝ

Bronson Ave.

Ⓟ

Ⓛ Ⓙ

Frost Ave.

Ⓜ

Seward St.

Bartlett St. Ⓗ

Ford St.

Reynolds St.

Jefferson Ave.

Exchange St.

Genesee St.

Ⓞ

S. Plymouth Ave.

River

Magnolia St.

Ⓘ

N

Ⓐ Former AME Zion Church
(42 Favor St.)
Ⓑ Former commercial center
(Spring St.)
Ⓒ Clarissa Street
Ⓓ Pythodd Club/Elks Lodge
(283-5 Clarissa St.)
Ⓔ Mt. Olivet Baptist Church
(141 Adams St.)
Ⓕ Jordan Home (136 Adams St.)

Ⓖ James and Bessie Hamm House
(301 Adams St.)
Ⓗ Cynthia Fitzpatrick Cooperative
(239-259 Reynolds St.)
Ⓘ Dett House (1087 S. Plymouth Ave.)
Ⓙ Mt. Zion Progressive Baptist
Church (131 Bronson Ave.)
Ⓚ Susan B. Anthony Home
(17 Madison St.)
Ⓛ Dorsey House (147 Bronson Ave.)
Ⓜ George Brown (77 Seward)
Ⓝ Dr. Van T. Levy (48 Glascow St.)
Ⓞ Latimer Funeral Home
(983 S. Plymouth Ave.)
Ⓟ Present AME Zion Church
(549 Clarissa St.)

Map courtesy of the Democrat and Chronicle and Times-Union

The West Side

The people and places found in the Third Ward are extremely important to the history of Rochester's African-American community. Rochester began on the west side of the Genesee River. Its first residential neighborhood was Corn Hill, located in the city's Third Ward. Often referred to as the "Ruffled Shirt" or "Silk Stocking District," Corn Hill served as the residence of choice for the city's mercantile, professional, and affluent families.

Atkinson St., an affluent residential street in the heart of Rochester's first neighborhood.

With the expansion of the old Rochester Institute of Technology campus, the Inner Loop highway system, and general urban renewal, many of the fine old homes have disappeared.

In the rest of the Third Ward, a thriving community of African-Americans served the affluent Corn Hill community as domestics and suppliers of other household help. African-Americans also found jobs downtown in businesses hotels, banks, restaurants, and with other employers eagerly seeking cheap labor. In this way, Rochester's African-Americans gained ready access to downtown Rochester and its affluent class early in the 19th century. It was within this west-side enclave that the social and service institutions would develop and serve the expanding African-American community. The side streets off the main thoroughfare that is now called Clarissa St., provided space for a number of these institutions, thus developing an almost self-contained community.

Former Memorial A.M.E. Zion Church. The former A.M.E. Zion Church is the oldest African-American church in Rochester. Originally located on Favor St., the congregation built three churches at that location before moving to its current location at 549 Clarissa St. For almost 75 years, this congregation, organized in 1827 and incorporated in 1839, was the major religious society for Rochester's African-American community.

The Memorial A.M.E. Zion Church, built in 1906 on Favor St., was spared during urban renewal because of its historic significance.

Courtesy of the City of Rochester

The first pastor, the Reverend Thomas James (1804-1891), purchased the Favor St. site. The original church on this site served as a station for the Underground Railroad, and Frederick Douglass printed his first issues of the *North Star* from its basement. A bronze bust honoring the Reverend Thomas James is located on the mezzanine level of the Public Safety Building in downtown Rochester. A new church was built in 1879. In 1906 the present brick church was constructed in the popular Romanesque Revival style, characterized by round arched windows and doorways, as well as a corbelled brick cornice and bell tower. In the 1906 structure, Susan B. Anthony and Frederick Douglass were memorialized with stained-glass windows. The Douglass window, donated by John W. Thompson, was destroyed in the early 1970s. However, the Anthony window survives in the present church on

18

Clarissa St. Susan B. Anthony gave one of her last lectures in the Favor St. church. Today the building is occupied by the Greater Bethlehem Temple Pentecostal Church.

From the early 1900s until the 1960s, directly opposite the former Memorial A.M.E. Zion Church, was a thriving residential and commercial enclave centered on Spring and Favor Streets. Benjamin and Vordie Hawkins (37 Favor St.) maintained a combination barber and beauty shop in their home; the second floor was used as dwelling space. This pattern was not uncommon in the business and commercial district that formed in this area of the Third Ward. On Spring St., the Stevens Store and Jentons Community Store, a combination soda parlor and restaurant, flourished in a community whose residents were generally unwelcome in the established enterprises downtown. Today, the former A.M.E. Zion Church is surrounded by highways and all of the commercial establishments and most of the residences have been demolished.

Clarissa Street, "Rochester's Broadway." Historically, most major cities had one thoroughfare or central business and social artery for its black community — Amsterdam Ave. in New York City, State St. in Chicago, Columbus Ave. in Boston. In Rochester, by the mid-20th century, it was Clarissa St. Originally known as High St. and later as Caledonia Ave., Clarissa St. became the center for social, cultural, and public life for African-Americans in Rochester's Third Ward.

It was this street that divided the wealth of the Corn Hill community from the less affluent who provided their domestic services. The small, modest, worker's houses sheltered the family and gave it proximity to employment in the mansions of Corn Hill as well as the business and commercial establishments of nearby downtown.

Clarissa St. provided an easy access to the African-American churches, physicians, and entertainment life not found in other sec-

Clarissa St., looking north from the corner of Edinburgh St.

Courtesy of the City of Rochester

Courtesy of Charles Price

tions of the city in equal abundance. Today, Clarissa St., a victim of urban renewal, no longer has the vibrancy of its earlier years yet retains something of its old flavor in establishments like Shep's and the Elks Club. On the following pages you'll read about the west side and its landmarks.

At the corner of Clarissa and Troup St. a Third Ward mansion became one of the high spots of Rochester nightlife for both blacks and whites. Jointly owned by the Knights of Pythias and the Odd Fellows lodges, the Pythodd Club originally was used by both organizations as a meeting place. Later a jazz club was added on the ground floor. In the 1950s this more expanded enterprise became the center for modern and progressive jazz music in Rochester, knowing no racial barriers.

Next door, again in a converted house (285 Clarissa St.), Elks Lodge #91 Flower City Chapter and Eldorado Temple #32 Auxiliary have maintained their headquarters. The Elks Lodge dates to 1906 and the Temple to 1907.

To complement the Elks and Pythodd Clubs was Joseph and Rebecca Daniels' "Dan's Restaurant and Grill" next door at number 293. "Dan" and Rebecca believed that the Rochester black community would support a high-quality, black-owned restaurant. His belief was well-founded, and although Dan's has passed on to new owners and renamed Shep's, it remains a tradition, offering high-quality entertainment.

Two Clarissa St. houses are significant in this area. The Joseph and Rebecca Daniels' home at 297 next door to "Dan's" was the first parsonage for any African-American church in the city. Purchased in 1910 with the aid of John W. Thompson, the two-story, two-bay, late

Jesse Stevens' Store, corner of Caledonia Ave. (Clarissa St.) and Spring Sts. (Below) Elizabeth "Bessie" Stevens Walls.

Courtesy of Charles Price

20

19th-century, vernacular, front-gable house — with simple stone sills and lintels and enclosed side porch — served as the home for pastors of Memorial A.M.E. Zion Church.

In the next block, at 351, was the Stevens house. This was the home of Rochester's longtime, only black public-school teacher, Elizabeth "Bessie" Stevens Walls. Mrs. Walls taught at George Mather Forbes School Number 4 on Bronson Ave.

Two, now demolished, structures on Clarissa St. were institutions for many years and now exist in new locations, one in a different format. The Colored YWCA founded in 1922, long stood at 192 Clarissa St., directly opposite the former site of the Millard E. Latimer Funeral Home. In 1949 that YWCA merged with the parent branch downtown. In 1961 it was restructured as the Montgomery Neighborhood Center, an independent social service agency, in a new facility at 10 Cady St.

Today, the funeral home, managed by Millard E. Latimer, Jr., is located at 983 Plymouth Ave. S. This business is Rochester's oldest black-owned enterprise.

The Mount Olivet Baptist Church, built in 1926 at 141 Adams St., is the second church built by this congregation. Founded in 1910, although meeting as early as 1908, the church was originally located on the rear of the parking lot to the east of the present building. Due to the popularity of Dr. James E. Rose, pastor

Lewis Bracey

Millard E. Latimer & Son Funeral Directors, Inc., 983 S. Plymouth Ave.

Courtesy of Rochester Public Library

Mt. Olivet Baptist Church, 141 Adams St.

from 1920-1942, the congregation grew, making the earlier building inadequate for the city's third-oldest black congregation. The first church building, now demolished, found use at one time as the colored or West Side YMCA, and later as a social center known as Hubert Hall. This building was razed after the educational building was added to the rear of the church in the mid-1960s.

The Mt. Olivet parsonage, now demolished, was a large, multiple- family dwelling at 137 Adams St. Many distinguished guests including Dr. Mordecai Johnson, president of Howard University, and Dr. Benjamin E. Mays, president of Morehouse College and a mentor of Dr. Martin Luther King, Jr. were housed there. It was within this house that the early local planning for what later became the United Negro College Fund was orchestrated.

9 Greenwood St., built in 1837, was the home of Mrs. Helen Murray Fish. It served as an informal drop-in center for the children of the Third Ward. Mrs. Fish purchased and restored this charming early 19th-century vernacular brick residence with carriage house and walled garden in 1940. Here, she introduced children to music, art, and taught them to respect themselves and others. When the Society of Friends purchased the house in 1947, Mrs. Fish, a Quaker, continued to live there. Mrs. Fish was also involved in the activities of the Montgomery Neighborhood Center and other community organizations.

Eventually, a need was recognized for a professionally run daycare center in the community. The Community Child Care Center was established in 1963 by Dr. G. Juanita Pitts, Rochester's first African-American female physician, at 858 Jefferson Ave. with the assistance of Kathryn Terrell and Addie Madison. For a time, the center was relocated to the Memorial A.M.E. Zion Church.

In 1975, the Community Child Care Center moved to its present location, a building at 170 Troup St. near Clarissa St. and designed by African-American architect Thomas W. Boyde, Jr. This building was financed partially through funds provided by Mrs. Fish, who died in 1967 at the age of 88. The Center's building is dedicated to her memory.

Women's Clubs. African-American women have been very active in clubs and self-help organizations since the 19th century. Mrs. Hester C. Jeffrey, a close friend and associate of Susan B.

Anthony, was an organizer of the National Association of Colored Women's Clubs (1895). Mrs. Jeffrey, the daughter-in-law of wealthy, politically active Rev. Roswell Jeffrey, also served as president of the State Federation of Colored Women's Clubs.

The present-day Rochester Federation of Women's Clubs was founded in 1930 by Mrs. Cullen Taylor. In 1948 it purchased its first clubhouse at 183 Adams St. Razed during urban renewal by the widening of Ford St., this organization was forced in 1969 to relocate to 616 Genesee St. Their clubhouse is a handsome example of turn-of-the-century Colonial Revival design, featuring a Palladian window, corner pilasters and full front porch with round columns.

The Hamm Home, 301 Adams St.

The James and Bessie Hamm home, built in 1888 at 301 Adams St., is an excellent example of west-side post-Civil War housing. Mr. and Mrs. Hamm had no children of their own but devoted their time and energy to helping young people prepare for productive lives. The Parents and Students Want to Know Group and the annual Ralph Bunche scholarships for high school graduates were two of the efforts the Hamms contributed to the community. The home, now a designated city landmark features both Eastlake and high Victorian Gothic influences, such as the elaborate chamfered porch posts, decorative gable woodwork and distinctive porch railing. It serves as a youth counseling center.

Cynthia Fitzpatrick Housing Cooperative. (Corner of Bartlett and Reynolds Streets.) Three buildings at this intersection comprise an important community housing project. Listed on the New York State and National Register of Historic Places— the O'Kane Market, 104-106 Bartlett St.; the O'Kane Building, 239-259 Reynolds St.; and the brick house, 237 Reynolds St. — have been refurbished as living quarters for 15 families all of whom will eventually own their own apartments. The O'Kane properties were originally developed as a commercial venture by two brothers. With its Queen Anne and Romanesque detailing, the building erected in 1889 at 239-259

The Cynthia Fitzpatrick Housing Cooperative, corner Bartlett and Reynolds Sts.

Reynolds St. originally included street-level housing and a second floor recreation hall. The adjacent building at 104-106 Reynolds St. is a handsome example of Italianate commercial design featuring an elaborate cast iron storefront.

This innovative project, among the first low-income cooperatives in western New York was named for Cynthia Fitzpatrick, believed to be Monroe County's oldest resident when she died at the age of 118 in 1983.

Respected for her wisdom and her age, she counseled neighborhood children at nearby Clara Barton School Number 2 on Reynolds St. As she grew older, Mrs. Fitzpatrick became increasingly known outside the neighborhood, making national news because of her longevity.

R. Nathaniel Dett. The spacious residence at 1087 South Plymouth Ave., with its Queen Ann styling and Colonial Revival details, was the Rochester home of the acclaimed musician and composer, R. Nathaniel Dett. Born in 1882 in Drummonderville (near Niagara Falls), Ontario, Canada, Dett, in 1932, was the first black person to receive a Bachelor of Music degree from the Eastman School of Music. A college professor and music teacher, he was a longtime director of music at Hampton Institute in Hampton, VA. (1913-31). It was his professional skill that developed the Hampton Institute Choir into an international organization. In 1919 he helped to found the National Association of Negro Musicians. He also served as music director for the United Service Organizations (USO) in Battle Creek, Michigan. He died in 1943.

Early 20th-century medical professionals on the west-side. The practice of medicine in Rochester has progressed considerably since the days of Drs. Harry Davis and John Jenkins. Actually, Rochester's small African-American community was well served during the early 20th century by talented professionals who lived on the west side of the city.

One significant physician was Dr. Charles T. Lunsford who practiced at 574 Clarissa St., now the site of the A.M.E. Zion Church. A president of the Rochester branch of the National Association for the Advancement of Colored People, he championed civil rights throughout the community long before there was a national movement. Dr. Lunsford also was instrumental in the racial integration of the University of Rochester's School of Medicine and Dentistry. School Number 19 on Seward St. is named for him, as is the traffic circle and urban park between Edinburgh and Glasgow Streets in the Corn Hill neighborhood. His home was at 90 Elmwood Ave. opposite Genesee Valley Park.

Dr. Anthony L. Jordan was a physician whose efforts on behalf of the poor were tireless. His office and home, at 136 Adams St., which he purchased in 1936 was built in 1875. He served the people day and night, welfare or paying patients, in a practice directed to the people of his community. Today, the Anthony L. Jordan Health Center, 82 Holland St,, stands as a tribute to his medical leadership of Rochester's minority community. In later years, Dr. Jordan resided at 400 Wellington Ave. in the 19th Ward.

Two dentists who served the community on the west side, were **Dr. J. Van Tuyl Levy** at 43 Glasgow St., and **Dr. Samuel A. Lindsay** at 115 West Main St. Dr. Lindsay also resided on the west side at 750 Arnett Blvd.

George Brown. As a slave, George Brown was sold for $1,450 at an auction in

George Brown in Grand Army of the Republic (G.A.R.) Civil War uniform. George Brown (left) with other veterans at Rochester parade, 1922.

Photos from the Stone Negative Collection, Rochester Museum & Science Center, Rochester, New York

1862. Brown had the distinction of serving both the Confederate and Union forces in the Civil War, as a body servant to a Confederate officer during the first part of the war and in a Union artillery regiment in the latter part.

Born in Culpeper County, VA, Mr. Brown moved to Rochester after living in Bradford, Pennsylvania. He died in 1940 at the age of 97. George Brown's home at 77 Seward St. is now the Friendship United Baptist Church.

Mt. Zion Progressive Missionary Baptist Church. This church, at 131 Bronson Ave., is noted for its stained-glass windows commemorative of many of Rochester's oldest black families. The edifice has housed at least four congregations since it was built in 1887. This Queen Anne style building is the most distinctive of the few small wood 19th-century churches remaining in the city. It includes a bell tower, bracketed entrance, and multiple stained-glass windows highlighted by the large rose window on the facade. The building was the home of Trinity Presbyterian Church from 1916 until 1971 when the congregation merged with the predominantly white Emmanuel Presbyterian Church and relocated to their church at 9 Shelter St. at the corner of Jefferson Ave. The stained-glass windows placed by Trinity's congregation, the second-oldest black church in the city, were not removed at the time of the merger.

Dorsey Home for Dependent Colored Children, 147 Bronson Ave. In 1910, Mrs. Isabella Dorsey began to care for orphaned black children in her home. Due to the lack of space, the orphanage moved to a small tract of land with one building in the Forest Lawn section of Sea Breeze. However, white neighbors began to develop a summer colony of cottages and objected to the presence of black children on the beach, thus necessitating another move. Through the generosity of local citizens, the Dorsey orphanage moved in 1918 to the 26-acre

Mt. Zion Progressive Missionary Baptist Church (formerly Trinity Presbyterian Church), built in 1887 on the corner of Bronson Ave. and Reynolds St.

Mrs. Isabella Dorsey cared for black orphaned children in her home.

Highland View Stock Farm on S. Clinton Ave. in Brighton. With changing social philosophies, the home was closed in 1928, and the children sent to their home communities where they were placed in private homes. McQuaid Jesuit High School now occupies the last site of the Dorsey Home.

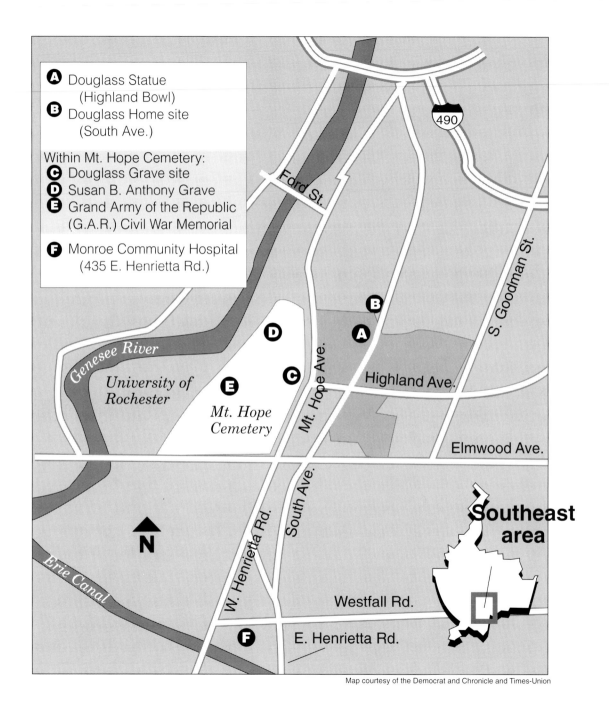

A Douglass Statue
(Highland Bowl)
B Douglass Home site
(South Ave.)

Within Mt. Hope Cemetery:
C Douglass Grave site
D Susan B. Anthony Grave
E Grand Army of the Republic
(G.A.R.) Civil War Memorial

F Monroe Community Hospital
(435 E. Henrietta Rd.)

490

Ford St.

S. Goodman St.

Genesee River

University of
Rochester

Mt. Hope
Cemetery

Mt. Hope Ave.

Highland Ave.

Elmwood Ave.

N

Erie Canal

W. Henrietta Rd.

South Ave.

Southeast
area

Westfall Rd.

E. Henrietta Rd.

Map courtesy of the Democrat and Chronicle and Times-Union

The Southeast

Frederick Douglass made his home near what is now Highland Park, which makes the southeast area of the city very important to the study of black sites in Rochester. Although there was not a large black population in the southeast, we can look here for reminders of Douglass, one of Rochester's most important historical figures of any race.

This section also includes information about Cab Calloway, who was born in the southeast, and about Thomas W. Boyde, Jr., Rochester's first black architect and designer of the outstanding Monroe Community Hospital complex.

Cab Calloway Marker. The most recent addition to African-American historic sites is the Cab Calloway marker in Otto Henderberg Square on Sycamore St. in the city's Swillburg neighborhood.

Born in Rochester on Christmas Day, 1907, Calloway's love of music came from hearing his mother sing and his aunt play the organ. An internationally acclaimed band leader, actor, dancer and composer, Calloway received an honorary doctorate from the University of Rochester and the 1993 National Medal of Arts at the White House from President Clinton.

The marker is located near 14 Sycamore St. where he once lived with his family and proclaims Cabell "Cab" Calloway the King of "Hi-De-Ho" from the chorus of his theme song, Minnie the Moocher.

Courtesy of the City of Rochester

Cab Calloway Marker on Sycamore St. in Rochester's Swillburg neighborhood.

The main entrance of Monroe Community Hospital overlooks the Erie Canal.

Thomas W. Boyde, Jr. In 1930, Thomas W. Boyde, Jr., an extraordinary young architectural graduate, came to Rochester to assist in the design of a new hospital after being hired by Siegmund J. Firestone, a local well-known architect. This event is noteworthy because Boyde, only 23 years old, became Rochester's first African-American architect. The hospital, Monroe County Home and Infirmary, has been recognized as a masterpiece, both as a social institution and as a work of architecture. Its innovative design and construction were way ahead of their time.

Siegmund J. Firestone was the architect for the Monroe County Home and Infirmary, while the young Thomas Boyde was one of several designers who worked with him on this large medical complex at 435 East Henrietta Road. Now known as Monroe Community Hospital, this Lombard Romanesque facility long ago lost its early image of "the poor farm." The exterior of the hospital, with its distinctive tile roof, features dragons, cherubs, grotesques, and gargoyles, with symbols of evil, good, and sickness combined with human figures.

After studying at Brown University, Boyde received an architectural degree from Syracuse University in 1928. While attending Syracuse University, he won a $1,500 award in a student drawing competition for an architectural rendering.

He was working in New York City when he answered Firestone's advertisement. Boyde remained with Firestone until 1933 and also worked for other firms in Rochester. Later he was a designer of fighter aircraft in a Buffalo defense plant. Boyde returned to Rochester in 1945. In 1947 he became self-employed, with Mr. Firestone helping him to meet prospective clients.

Boyde's contributions to the Rochester area are many, including several former Star Markets, the Woodie View Apartments at 1835 St. Paul Boulevard, the Community Child Care Center at 170 Troup Street, and many suburban homes, churches, and small commercial buildings. In Boyde's later years, he looked back fondly upon his exterior design contributions to his first Rochester project, the Monroe Community Hospital. He also took special pride in the many suburban residences he designed.

The Rochester Museum and Science Center currently is researching and cataloging many of Boyde's plans and drawings, for as his friend William J. Knox has stated: "His talents made it possible for him to make his living purely as an architect," an unusual feat for an African-American prior to World War II.

The Frederick Douglass Memorial Square. Located in Rochester's world-famous Highland Park, with its unsurpassed collection of lilacs, this square is now home to the relocated Frederick Douglass monument.

In 1898, after a painful period of fund-raising and several years of planning and organizing, a monument to Frederick Douglass was dedicated and placed on a plot of land named Frederick Douglass Park at St. Paul St. and Central Ave., near the New York Central Railroad Station in the city's northeast side. John W. Thompson was instrumental in organizing a committee to build a monument. In this endeavor Thompson solicited and received support from Rochester's prominent citizens as well as from other parts of the country.

Gordon Ball

The Frederick Douglass Statue was originally located at the intersection of St. Paul St. and Central Ave.

Now at Highland Park, the Frederick Douglass Monument faces north.

A longtime activist in the black community, Thompson arrived in Rochester in 1883. He was a messenger for the attorney general's office which required frequent trips to Albany. He had also held positions as a waiter and a clerk. He became a devoted member of the Douglass League and Eureka Lodge Number 36, Free and Accepted Masons. When a monument to Civil War soldiers and sailors was proposed for Washington Square Park, Thompson began to interest the black community in erecting a monument for African-American Civil War soldiers. As these plans were being formulated, Frederick Douglass, long-time former Rochester resident, died on February 20, 1895, in Washington, D.C.

It appeared to be logical that Douglass' adopted hometown should recognize this local hero for his extraordinary contribution to emancipation, women's suffrage, and civil rights. Thompson soon began the campaign for financing an appropriate symbol of recognition for Douglass. A committee was organized, and funds were sought.

The Douglass monument was the first public monument dedicated to an African-American in the United States. Douglass' son, Charles, posed for this work by sculptor Sidney W. Edwards.

With the deterioration of the Central Ave. area, which had become smoky and congested, civic concern brought about the decision to relocate the monument to a more desirable site. The monument was relocated to Highland Park and rededicated in Sept., 1941, with the appropriate Masonic exercises of Eureka Lodge Number 36. Douglass faces north, thus fulfilling a concern of his friend and colleague in social reform, Susan B. Anthony, who stated in 1899, "I wonder how the mistake was made of having it face the South. It ought not be so and I shall endeavor to have it changed. He always faced North; his paper was called *The North Star*, and I do not like to see him look to the South."

The Frederick Douglass Home Site. Frederick Douglass' home was located on the site of James P.B. Duffy School 12, (999 South Ave.), in the block to the north of his statue in Highland Park. Douglass occupied this house with his family in an attempt to find personal safety after the Fugitive Slave Law was passed in 1850. His home, in what was then the countryside, frequently housed fugitive slaves and was visited by fiery abolitionist, John Brown. While Douglass was traveling in 1872, leaving his family at home, the house was torched and destroyed. Ironically, Douglass once said of Rochester, "I shall always feel more at home there than anywhere else in the country."

Mt. Hope Cemetery

Mount Hope Cemetery was dedicated on October 3, 1838, and is the oldest municipally owned Victorian cemetery in America. Through the years it has increased in size through land acquisition. Many records of interment were lost in 1857 during the administration of city comptroller John B. Robertson. While some records were subsequently found in Canada, official records remain incomplete. This cemetery, unlike those in some other communities, was never segregated. Therefore, the resting places of African-Americans are located in every corner of the grounds.

Following are some prominent Rochesterians of African-American descent who are buried in Mt. Hope Cemetery. Some of these people are buried in unmarked graves. To visit any of these sites, ask for directions at the cemetery office.

Frederick Douglass Family Plot. Rochester's most revered African-American, Frederick Douglass, is buried in Mount Hope Cemetery. His resting place is marked by a black granite memorial and a tablet near a white wrought-iron resting bench. This is a family plot and includes his first wife, Anna Murray Douglass (1882), and daughter, Annie (1860). Douglass' second wife, Helen Pitts Douglass (1903), is also entombed here. Note the discrepancy in dates on the marker and tablet. Douglass thought that he had been born in 1817; however, scholars have discovered documents indicating his actual

Courtesy of the City of Rochester

Frederick Douglass family plot overlooks Highland Ave.

Black and white Civil War veterans rest side by side in the G.A.R. Memorial plot.

birthdate to be 1818. The granite marker was placed by sons, Lewis and Charles Douglass, both veterans of the Civil War serving in the all-black Massachusetts 54th Regiment.

Grand Army of the Republic (G.A.R.) Civil War Memorial. Veterans of the Civil War are memorialized in a plot at the end of Grove Ave. in the extreme western part of the cemetery. Here may be found the graves of African-Americans who fought in that conflict. Several are identified as having been in "colored" units.

United Sons of Rochester. This plot was purchased in 1849 by an association of African-Americans. The records of this group have disappeared, possibly in 1857 when many cemetery records were lost. Three small stones mark its width. The gravestone that marks the plot is D. E. Wycoff. The names and numbers of persons interred here are unknown.

Several other people who were important in shaping the history of Rochester are buried in the Mt. Hope Cemetery. Women's suffragette, Susan B. Anthony, long-time friend of Frederick Douglass and co-laborer in the anti-slavery movement, made her home in Rochester at 17 Madison St. She also rests in Mount Hope Cemetery, a short distance north of the Douglass plot. Listed here are a few of these people and their achievements:

Caudilla L. Baker. Mr. Baker was the manager of Hanover Houses, Rochester's first low-income housing project. Hanover Houses was the result of the city's attempt in the 1950s to revitalize the Baden-Ormond St. neighborhood. Born in Klondike, Texas, Mr. Baker died in Rochester in 1983 at the age of 75. A scholarship funded by relatives and administered by the Rochester Area United Nations memorializes his work with that organization.

Dr. Bertrand M. Boddie. The second African-American to graduate from the University of Rochester School of Medicine and Dentistry (1951), Dr. Boddie practiced medicine at 254 and 580

Joseph Ave. and later became the first black physician for the Eastman Kodak Company (1973-1988). Dr. Boddie also was the first black president of the New York State Chapter of the American Heart Association. Dr. Boddie died in October, 1990.

Thomas W. Boyde, Jr. Rochester's first African-American architect rests in an unmarked grave. Mr. Boyde moved to Rochester in 1930 and practiced until his death in 1981.

Reverend Frank L. Brown. A native of Jamaica, Father Brown was the founding pastor of St. Simon's Episcopal Church and led it for 18 years. This African-American church merged with St. Luke's Episcopal Church in 1988. Father Brown died in 1948.

Leon J. Du Bois. Leon Du Bois arrived in Rochester in 1888 from Fulton County, New York where he was born in 1865. A leader in the Trinity Presbyterian Church, he also served as chaplain for Eureka Lodge No. 36 F.&A.M. He was one of the original planners of the Frederick Douglass monument and participated in the laying of the cornerstone in 1898. He died in 1948.

Cynthia Fitzpatrick. The daughter of enslaved parents, Mrs. Fitzpatrick was at the time of her death in 1983 thought to be 118 years old, the oldest person in the Rochester area. Generous with her time to the neighborhood children, she is memorialized by the Cynthia Fitzpatrick Cooperative Housing Project a few blocks from her home. She is buried in an unmarked grave. Mrs. Fitzpatrick died in 1983.

Reverend Thomas James. The founding pastor of Memorial A.M.E. Zion Church is in an unmarked grave. A former slave, he made his home in Rochester. Born in Canajoharie, New York, in 1804, while slavery was still legal in the state, he died in Rochester in 1891.

Reverend Roswell D. Jeffrey. Born in 1805 in Lyme, CT., Rev. Jeffrey was a businessman and owned land bounded by East Ave.,

Courtesy of the Rochester Public Library

The Rev. Frank L. Brown (left) assists Episcopal Bishop David Lincoln Ferris (center) in laying the cornerstone for St. Simon's Church.

Monroe Ave., Meigs St. and Goodman St. Also an ordained minister, he had charges in Albion, Geneva and Canandaigua. He was the eighth pastor of the Memorial A.M.E. Zion Church. Mr. Jeffrey died at his home on Meigs St. in 1890.

Dr. Anthony L. Jordan. Known as "doctor to the poor," Dr. Jordan, an African-South American, practiced medicine in the Third Ward at 136 Adams St. from 1932 until his death in 1971. The Anthony L. Jordan Health Center is named in his memory.

Millard E. Latimer. The Millard E. Latimer and Son Funeral Home is Rochester's oldest black-owned business. Mr. Latimer (1895-1980) was for many years the financial clerk of the Mount Olivet Baptist Church.

John G. Lee. Active in the African-American life of Rochester, Mr. Lee was employed by the former Lincoln Rochester Trust Company for 50 years prior to his retirement in 1951. He was a member of the Board of Managers of the West Side YMCA and a Sunday School superintendent of the Memorial A.M.E. Zion Church. Mr. Lee was also a past master of Eureka Lodge of Masons, Prince Hall Affiliate. John G. Lee lived on Garson Ave. in a house that is still standing. He died in 1960 at the age of 88.

Dr. Samuel A. Lindsay. Rochester's second African-American dentist practiced in the West Main St./Plymouth Ave. area. A native of Augusta, Georgia, he came to Rochester in 1918. He worked as a waiter at the Powers Hotel in Rochester to pay his way through Lincoln University in Pennsylvania and the School of Dentistry at Howard University. In 1925 he opened his first office. His home, purchased in 1937, was on Arnett Blvd. in the 19th Ward.

James McCuller. A community activist for 25 years in Rochester, Mr. McCuller was executive director of the anti-poverty agency, Action for a Better Community. An outspoken advocate for minorities and the poor, he led marches to end violence and reduce the city's homicide rate. Born in Arkansas, McCuller came to Rochester in 1961. He died in 1992.

Jacob Morris. A barber and civic leader, Morris assisted Frederick Douglass in processing fugitive slaves through Rochester into Canada. Morris died in 1866.

Dr. Edwin A. Robinson. Dr. Robinson was the first African-American to graduate (1945) from the University of Rochester School of Medicine and Dentistry. A physician, he lived on E. Henrietta Road and served two terms as president of the Highland Hospital medical staff. He died in 1972.

Dr. James E. Rose. For 22 years (1920-42), Dr. Rose served as pastor of the Mount Olivet Baptist Church. A graduate of Howard University and Rochester Theological Seminary, he planned and oversaw the construction of the Gothic, vaulted ceiling edifice on Adams St. Dr. Rose died in 1942.

Stanley J. Thomas, Sr. Mr. Thomas was the first African-American to hold a major position in Rochester city government. He was appointed Director of Sanitation in 1962. A native of Binghamton, New York (1899) he came to Rochester in 1930. He also served as assistant to the Public Works commissioner. Mr. Thomas died in 1992.

The Northeast

This community has a history of ethnic richness. Beginning as a German Jewish enclave in the 1840s, the area later became the Seventh Ward, bordering the New York Central railroad tracks, which separated it from the rest of the community. At one time, the area was known as Dublin, because of its Irish population. However, the increasing number of other ethnic groups changed the character of the area.

By the turn of the century, the Jewish immigrant population was so large that it eventually petitioned City Council to change the name of St. Joseph St. to Joseph Ave. The area today is predominantly African-American and Hispanic. However, this community's architecture, along with its adaptations, reflects a vibrant community reminiscent of the culture of those generations of people which have called the district home.

Full Gospel Tabernacle Church, 6 Oregon St. Responding to an ever increasing African-American population with an interest in the Anglican Church tradition, St. Simon's Mission was established in 1928. Under the leadership of Reverend Frank L. Brown, the 60 member mission moved into the building at 6 Oregon St. becoming St. Simon's Episcopal Church in January, 1935. The church, a Colonial Revival style with recessed portico and decorative entrance, was designed by noted architect J. Foster Warner, who presented the plans as a gift to the congregation. The building was constructed on the former site of Wagner College which later moved to Staten

(Above) St. Simon's Episcopal Church, 8 Oregon St.

(Right) Church of God and Saints of Christ, 30 Leopold St.

Island, NY.

In 1943 the parish purchased 192 Ormond St., which had previously housed the Hebrew Free Library. They renamed it the Carver House in honor of the noted black chemist, Dr. George Washington Carver, who had died a year earlier, and the late Reverend Charles C. W. Carver, longtime rector of Christ Church. For many years the Carver House served as a center for social, cultural, and recreational activities in the black community. The church sold the building in 1951. Sommerville Printing Company now occupies a building that surrounds the Carver House, but by looking carefully you can still see the second floor and attic.

In 1952 the congregation built a parish house designed to complement the church's architecture. It served the same function that the Carver House had served but was directly adjacent to the church.

In January, 1988, St. Simon's Church merged with St. Luke's Episcopal Church, a predominantly white congregation at 17 South Fitzhugh St. The stained-glass windows and altar in the chapel were lovingly removed from St. Simon's and reinstalled in St. Luke's chapel. This new, merged congregation is now known as the Church of St. Luke and St. Simon Cyrene, and worships in the 1823 former St. Luke's Church, the oldest public building in Rochester.

The Church of God and Saints of Christ, 30 Leopold St. One block from St. Simon's, this congregation occupies the former Beth Israel Synagogue, built in 1886 for the Orthodox congregation founded in 1874. The present congregation, which purchased the building in 1973, observes the Saturday Sabbath, Passover, and other Jewish practices in addition to

Christian teachings. The building is designed in the Romanesque style, which was frequently used for synagogues in Europe and the U.S. during the middle and late 19th century. This brick building with raised stone foundation is highlighted by the distinctive facade that includes round-arched windows, a center canopied entrance with paired cast iron stair cases, terra cotta cornice banding and copper fascia on the central arched pediment. The building was listed on the National Register of Historic Places in 1974.

Baden St. Settlement House, 152 Baden St. This social and cultural agency was founded in 1900 and incorporated in 1901. The agency was actually a continuation of an earlier organization, the Girls' Home Association then located on East Ave. The Baden St. Settlement House has serviced generations of immigrants and newcomers to Rochester in this culturally diverse neighborhood. Non-sectarian and socially aware of community needs, Baden St. Settlement House has been a significant part of African-American life through a variety of programs and services.

Coursesy of Millard E. Latimer, Jr.

Latimer and Myers Funeral Home. One indicator of the widening disbursement of the black community throughout Rochester was the establishment in 1924 of this business located in a private house in a predominantly white neighborhood at 638 Bay St. at the corner of Baycliff Drive. By 1930 Millard Latimer had moved to the west side, and opened his own business on Clarissa St.

Latimer and Myers Funeral Home, corner of Bay St. and Baycliff Dr., circa 1925.

Walter R. Myers remained in the northeast quadrant. After WW II (1947), Myers moved his funeral business to 14 Oregon St. The private home at 638 Bay St., which once served as the Latimer and Myers Funeral Home, is still standing.

Freddie Thomas. Born in 1918, Thomas was a leader in the black community, a biologist, and an inventor. He did extensive

Mildred Johnson

research in genetics and plastic surgery. His personal library contained over 5,400 books which he used for his international research, informal tutoring of students, and with visiting scholars. After his death in 1974, the Freddie Thomas Foundation was established in his memory. A significant expression of continuing Thomas' humanitarian work is the Freddie Thomas Scholarship Award for honor students in mathematics and science.

Another foundation project is the "Miss Jane Pittman Fountain," located downtown at Franklin St. and Liberty Pole Way. Situated on Liberty Pole Plaza, the drinking fountain represents human thirst for knowledge and understanding. The name of the fountain was chosen from the fictional character created by author Ernest Gaines.

Mildred W. Johnson. Born in Brighton, NY, in 1912, Mildred W. Johnson was a social activist and champion of the poor in Rochester. She was a member of the Rochester Chapter of the National Association for the Advancement of Colored People, Action for a Better Community (the anti-poverty agency), and founder of the Virginia Wilson Interracial and Helping Hands Center, named for her mother. The Center was dedicated to feeding, clothing, and housing the poor. Many times the homeless stayed in her home at 46 Farbridge St., between Remington St. and Joseph Ave. Johnson died at age 80 in August, 1992 and is buried in Riverside Cemetery.

The Migrants: From Culpeper, Virginia and Sanford, Florida to Rural Rochester

A hallmark of the African-American community to the Rochester area has been a succession of group migrations, each of which has contributed to the cultural and economic life of the community. Beginning with the manumission of the dozen or so former slaves of city founder Nathaniel Rochester, these free blacks mingled with the arrival of fugitives to form an early viable community.

These growth patterns were established in the areas surrounding Rochester. The greatest growth appears to be the result of what has been called the "Culpeper Connection." Legend maintains that Captain Frank Harmon was stationed for a time during the Civil War in the Culpeper, VA, area. After the war, he persuaded groups of newly freed men to migrate to the Mumford-Caledonia area, to work on his and other farms in the area.

Over a period of time many of these freed men acquired their own farms and, with continued migration, families were reunited and communities developed. Churches and social institutions were established, and some continue to prosper. Many Rochester area residents today trace their family roots to these early settlers from Culpeper, VA.

The Second Baptist Church, Mumford, NY. Founded by Reverend Clayton Coles in 1891, this church, located at 957 George St. in Mumford, was incorporated as the Belcoda Baptist Church of Mumford. The present name was adopted in 1944. Reverend Coles was born in slavery in 1838, and during the Civil War he became a body servant to General Stonewall Jackson. During this time he learned to read and write. Mordecai Johnson, the future president of Howard University in Washington, D.C., served the church as pastor from 1913 - 1916. The church continues to be a significant part of the community in Mumford. In 1934 Reverend Coles' grandson, Howard W. Coles, founded the *Frederick Douglass Voice*, a powerful publication for the black community. *The Frederick Douglass Voice* continues to publish today.

The Second Baptist Church, Le Roy, NY. This church, located at 73 Myrtle St. in Genesee County, while younger than the Mumford church, serves a population similar to its neighbor in Monroe County. The Second Baptist Church in Le Roy was founded by Dr. James E. Rose, who would later pastor Mount Olivet Baptist Church in Rochester for 22 years (1920 -1942). After graduation from the Rochester Theological Seminary (Colgate-Rochester Divinity School) in 1916, he pastored both the Mumford and Le Roy churches simultaneously. A native of Centreville, VA, he obviously had a special relationship with this preponderance of former Virginians and their descendants.

Johnson Park. Scottsville, one of the communities developed by blacks from Culpeper, is the home of the only public park in the area dedicated to an African-American. The park, named for the property's original owner, Stonewall Jackson Johnson, whose homestead is nearby, is a focal point for summer social activities. A baseball field, slides, and swings make this a pleasant sanctuary for local residents. Located on Main St. in the village, it has no historic marker.

The Sanford Arrivals. Blacks began to arrive in nearby Wayne County in 1931. The Fish brothers of Sodus employed an agent to recruit black workers for their packing house. The first crew numbered 25. By the late 1930s the crews grew to two per year and numbered 75. Today, Wayne County employs the largest migrant labor force of any county in New York State.

Many of the transplanted Sanfordites never returned to their homes but continued to live in the rural farming communities of Wayne County forming a "Sanford, Florida" community in the greater Rochester area. Eventually, the lack of employment in Wayne County forced many of the migrants and their descendents to seek work in Rochester. With this post World War II influx, the city's black population began to increase. This population movement was later augmented by the national movement of southern blacks to northern cities for greater industrial and commercial opportunities.

The Story Continues

In the 1840s Frederick Douglass found Rochester, then in its boomtown heyday, to be one of the country's most progressive cities. Prosperity and age may have blunted this progressive spirit. One hundred years later Rochester earned the sobriquet, "smugtown." Part of the smugness showed itself in a general lack of awareness of the needs of Rochester's growing black community.

It was not until World War II, when manpower for the defense efforts and federal legislation forbade racial discrimination in government contracts, that positions in Rochester's industrial community were reluctantly opened to African-Americans.

Another factor was the returning veterans who were restive and refused to accept second-class citizenship after fighting for democracy on foreign soil. The local returning service men and women soon were joined by their southern brothers and sisters who refused to return to state and locally sanctioned discrimination in their native South.

Unlike the earlier migration after World War I, Rochester began to witness a dramatic change in African-American population, and an emerging accommodation to the new arrivals. With each influx of new residents, the community became increasingly heterogeneous. States and communities of origin have brought diverse lifestyles and traditions. Rochester's African-American population continued to grow; by 1960, 23,586 blacks called the city home. In July, 1964, violence broke out in Rochester's black community, leading the nation into what would become a summer of urban unrest throughout the United States. From the 24th to the 26th, in the hottest July since 1955, four deaths and almost 1,000 arrests focused attention on the needs of black citizens, serious needs that had gone mainly unattended by government, civic leaders, and educators. Rochester would recover, but it would never be the same.

In the years that followed, professionals began to take positions of leadership at levels heretofore unimaginable in the Flower City. Dr. William Knox, Jr., a leader in the Manhattan Project that developed the atomic bomb, joined the Eastman Kodak Company as a research chemist. He was later joined by Dr. Walter Cooper, also a chemist. Dr. Cooper later became a regent of the University of the State of New York, the highest level of educational leadership in the state. William Warfield, a graduate of the Eastman School of Music achieved outstanding success as a Broadway performer and college professor and voice teacher. These pioneers and others infused local youth with black pride, the need for an educated citizenry and a demand for civil rights. In 1948 Charles H. Price became Rochester's first African-American police officer and later the first to achieve the rank of captain.

Communication has always been an important element within the black community. That heritage extended from the middle 19th century with Frederick Douglass and his newspaper, *The North Star*, to Howard Coles, his *Frederick Douglass Voice*, and his radio broadcasting career at radio station WSAY. Today, that same heritage is seen in the black-owned radio station WDKX (named for Frederick Douglass. Martin Luther King, Jr., and Malcolm X) and its owner, Andrew Langston. The circa 1880 Queen Anne-style house located at 683 East Main St., just outside the Inner Loop, was renovated by the Langstons and is an excellent example of an adaptive commercial reuse of a former residence.

Politically, progress has been made. Constance Mitchell was elected to the Monroe County Board of Supervisors in the early 1960s, the first African-American to serve in that body. Reuben Davis was appointed a City Court judge, Teresa D. Johnson became the first African-American woman appointed a City Court judge and

Truman Coles was appointed an assistant district attorney. The mayoral election of 1993 made history when both political parties fielded black candidates for mayor of the city of Rochester.

The city matured as the black population increased. By 1970 it had reached 49,647; in 1980 it was 62,332. The 1990 U.S. Census showed a black population of 73,102 or 31.5% of the city's 231,636 residents. Although blacks only comprised about 30 percent of the city's population, William A. Johnson, Jr. won the Democratic primary. In defeating several well-known political figures, Johnson became the first black mayor of Rochester, taking office on January 1, 1994 as the city's 64th mayor. The African-American community today is a vital part of the total community. The legacy of leadership that produced the institutions that have survived generations is healthy and poised for the future.

Additional Reading

Blassingame, John W. ed. *The Frederick Douglass Papers*, Vols. 1 and 2.
New Haven: Yale University Press, 1982.

Douglass, Frederick. *Life and Times of Frederick Douglass.*
New York: Grosset and Dunlap, Inc., 1970.

Douglass, Frederick. *My Bondage and My Freedom.*
New York: Dover Publications, Inc., 1969.

Dupree, Adolph. "Rochester Roots/Routes," *About...Time* magazine,
Vol. XII, Nos. 7-12, July-Dec., 1984.

Huggins, Nathan Irvin. *Slave and Citizen—The Life of Frederick Douglass.*
Boston: Little, Brown and Company, 1980.

Jacobs, Harriet A. *Incidents in the Life of a Slave Girl.*
New York: Harcourt Brace
Cambeidge: Harvard University Press, 1987.

James, Thomas. *Wonderful, Eventful Life of Rev. Thomas James.*
Rochester: Post-Express Printing Company, 1887.

Kobrin, David. *The Black Minority in Early New York.*
Albany: The University of the State of New York, 1971.

McFeely, William S. *Frederick Douglass.*
New York: W.W. Norton and Company, 1991.

McKelvey, Blake. "Lights and Shadows in Local Negro History."
Rochester History, Vol. XXI; No. 4, Oct., 1959.

Schmitt, Victoria Sandwick. "Goin' North," *Rochester History*,
Vol.LIV; No. 1, Winter, 1992.

Steward, Austin. *Twenty-two years a Slave, and Forty Years a Freeman.*
Rochester: W. Alling, 1856.

Whitaker, Arthur L. "Anatomy of a Riot." *The Crisis*, Vol. 72; No 1., Jan., 1965;
pp. 20-25.